Original title:
Pollination Poems

Copyright © 2025 Creative Arts Management OÜ
All rights reserved.

Author: Lucas Harrington
ISBN HARDBACK: 978-1-80566-616-5
ISBN PAPERBACK: 978-1-80566-901-2

Lullabies Among the Petals

In the garden, bees do buzz,
Sipping nectar, oh what a fuss.
They dance in circles, whirl and twirl,
A honey dance in a floral swirl.

Ladybugs laugh on leaves so neat,
While ants march on with tiny feet.
Caterpillars munch, with a munch and a crunch,
Turning into butterflies, oh what a bunch!

Bumblebees wear their fuzzy suits,
As they flirt with flowers, oh what a hoot!
Daisy and Rose play hide and seek,
While violets giggle, both mild and meek.

Oh, to be a petal in the breeze,
With buzzing pals, and a life of ease.
They hum a tune, a sweet serenade,
In lullabies where no one is frayed!

Melodies of the Meadow

A bee with a bowtie hums a tune,
Dancing flowers sway under the moon.
Butterflies quip, with jokes in the air,
As daisies giggle, without a care.

A ladybug prances, her spots all aglow,
She tells all the bugs, 'Come on, let's go!'
The ants form a conga, all in a line,
Marching on forward, feeling just fine.

Enchantment in Every Flutter

In the garden, bees wear shades of cool,
They buzz all around, like a winged school.
While flowers gossip, they trade little puns,
'Why did the bee buzz? It wanted some fun!'

A butterfly winks, with a flash of bright hue,
'I'm here for a party, who's joining the crew?'
The blooms laugh and cheer, in a colorful spree,
Together they dance, as wild as can be!

Spring's Choreographed Awakening

The dance of the drone, he's got some great moves,
Pollen partners whirl, finding their grooves.
Bees wear their crowns, they're royalty here,
Making sweet nectar while sipping on cheer!

A bumblebee twirls, then does a grand leap,
He'll flip and he'll flop, not missing a beat.
The blossoms all cheer, 'This show is so grand!'
Join in the fun, come lend a winged hand!

Garden of Pollinators' Dreams

In a garden of laughs, where the sun always shines,
   Moths tell tall tales, while sipping on wines.
   Grasshoppers chuckle, their legs all a-jump,
They leap through the daisies, a whimsical thump.

    Ladybugs play cards, just under a leaf,
'Go fish,' they giggle, with tongue-in-cheek grief.
The blooms tease the bugs, with a wink and a nod,
'Your dance moves are funny, but give them a prod!'

A Garden's Breath of Life

In a garden where flowers prance,
A bee sidesteps in a joyful dance.
With pollen pants, it zooms around,
Not a single petal's safe or sound.

It hovers near a daffodil,
"Excuse me, miss, I'll take my fill!"
The flowers giggle as he chats,
"Can you please stop wearing my hats?"

Caught in a tangle, what a sight,
The bee's stuck in a flower's tight light.
"Oh dear, this isn't what I planned!"
He whispers, while shoving pollen in hand.

But off he goes with a big, wide grin,
Leaving behind a ruckus and spin.
All the blooms cheer as he takes flight,
In this garden, life feels just right.

Flight Path of the Curious Bee

Buzzing through the morning mist,
This bee has a plot, you can't resist.
He wants a sip from each bright flower,
What a day, oh, what a power!

He zig-zags past a lavender bush,
"Hey there, pretty, don't you rush!"
But landing's tricky; oops, he missed!
"Hey, hold still! That was my twist!"

With nectar dreams that tempt the best,
The bee's a clumsy little guest.
"Excuse me, blooms, I'm here for lunch!"
But nature laughs louder with every crunch.

Yet still he bumbles, never meek,
In search of goodies, he's quite the freak.
And off he goes, a tiny astronaut,
In the humor of life, he's always caught!

Swaying in the Evening Breeze

As the sun sets, the garden sways,
A bee still buzzing through soft arrays.
"I'll take a break, just one quick sip!"
But oh, the petals make his trip!

In twilight's glow, he plays a game,
A dizzy waltz, is he insane?
"Just a nibble, do let me stay!"
A flower chuckles, "Sure, but no way!"

Through alleys of daisies, he drifts along,
Unaware he's caught in a floral song.
A butterfly giggles, "You're quite the clown!"
In their ballet, they twirl around.

Yet as he sways and tips his hat,
He finds a friend in a friendly cat.
Together they laugh, a sight so rare,
In this evening breeze, life's a fair!

Echoes of the Colorful Winged

Amidst blossoms of every shade,
Bees are buzzing, never swayed.
In frolic and fun, they make their mark,
Throwing flower parties, lighting the dark.

"Let's gather here, you bright little crew,
With giggly blooms and skies so blue!"
Said one bee wearing shades so fine,
"Join us now, it's party time!"

Petals nodding, swaying in glee,
"Who knew gardening could be so free?"
As they mix and mingle, laughter's the call,
A buzzing tango; they're having a ball!

So here's to the winged and those who thrive,
Creating chaos, making us alive.
With every buzz, we smile and cheer,
In the garden's stage, we all draw near!

Symphony of the Sunlit Blooms

Bees wear suits, all dressed in stripes,
Buzzing tunes with their tiny pipes.
Flowers dance, they sway and groove,
In this garden, they've got the moves.

Ladybugs join the funny show,
Twirling 'round like they know how to flow.
Sunshine beams on this merry crew,
Laughter grows, as petals renew.

A dandelion giggles at the sight,
With fluffy seeds taking off in flight.
Bees chase dreams on the wind's good cheer,
In this symphony, joy's crystal clear.

So grab a drink from the floral vase,
Join the bees in this cheerful race.
Under the sun's golden rays we bask,
Short jokes bloom, just for a laugh's task.

Nectar's Hidden Reverie

In a daisy's heart, a secret lies,
Sweet nectar's treasure, oh what a prize!
Bees doze off, in a flower's lap,
Dreaming of honey, in a sweet nap.

Bumblebee stumbles, a bit too bold,
Trips on a petal, now that's pure gold!
Waves to the ants, who laugh till they're sore,
"Hey, what's the buzz? We're all wanting more!"

Butterflies giggle, they flutter and tease,
Spreading the joy, like a summer breeze.
They paint the sky with colors so bright,
In this nectar dream, everything feels right.

So here's to the blooms who sing and sway,
They keep us laughing throughout the day.
As bees spill secrets and dance in delight,
Join in the fun, it's a flowery night!

Flutter Beneath the Petal's Veil

Beneath a flower, the critters collide,
With giggles and wiggles, they won't hide.
A tiny ant throws a wild dance,
While ladybugs cheer, giving him a chance.

Did you hear the flower make a joke?
It cracked a petal, oh what a poke!
Bees chuckle softly, sipping their brew,
In this garden club, we all feel new.

The raindrops giggle, they fall in line,
Tap-dancing on leaves like they're sipping wine.
A worm sings low, "I'm happy down here,"
While flowers burst out in cheerful cheer.

Together they twirl, this merry brigade,
Crafting a party that won't ever fade.
So lift your voice and join their spree,
In blooming laughter, we all feel free!

The Bee's Sacred Journey

A bee with a mission, flying high,
Winks at the flowers passing by.
"Hey there, pals! Got nectar to steal!
Just share a smile, that's the deal!"

He bumps a butterfly, oh what a sight,
They spin and giggle, what pure delight!
"Let's race to that bloom, it's ripe for the pluck,
In this pollen game, we're really in luck!"

While chasing the sun, they lose track of time,
Sipping sweet drinks, oh isn't it sublime?
A tiny bee says, "I could do this all day,
As long as there's laughter, I'm here to play!"

So here's to the flowers that line the way,
And bees who buzz in their silly ballet.
Join the journey, where giggles flow,
In fields of joy, let your spirits glow!

Whirling through Sunlit Orchards

Bumblebees buzzing like tiny bands,
They dance and dart with their tiny hands.
Orchards awake, the blossoms sway,
In a bright, sweet world, they steal the day.

Pollen on toes, they wear it with pride,
With every spin, the petals collide.
A little bee crashes, a bloom gives a laugh,
"Hey buddy, chill, you're not on a staff!"

Honey nectar dreams made on a whim,
Their tiny legs kick like they're in a gym.
As sunbeams play hide-and-seek up above,
These fuzzy fellows are fun, oh so tough!

With a twist and a twirl, they conquer the scene,
Like bees at a party, all dressed in green.
Each flower a friend, there's gossip to share,
"Who wore it best? Let's all stop and stare!"

The Dance of Wings and Stems

Wings flapping wildly, oh what a sight,
Tiny dancers performing in flight.
A symphony buzzing, it's a grand parade,
In this floral club, no favors are paid.

Stems sway and shake to the buzzing beat,
As flowers all cheer with their visual treat.
"More pollen, more fun," they cry with delight,
While butterflies swoop, lifting hearts to new heights.

A bumble spins out in a goofy trance,
With petals as partners, they all join the dance.
Buzzing with joy, it's a festival scene,
In this wacky garden, everyone's keen!

Among vibrant blooms, it's laughter galore,
Bees chat in whispers, and bugs share the floor.
They twirl with abandon, in sun and in shade,
In a world full of color, no one's afraid!

Nectar Trails in a Prism of Color

A rainbow of petals shines bright in the air,
While bees hold their cups, life's nectar they share.
With sugary sips and a flick of their wings,
They bring forth the laughter that nature all brings.

Tiny explorers on sweet sugar quests,
Joking with flowers, all dolled up in vests.
"Hey, is that nectar? Guess it's time for a feast!"
Flowers reply, "I'm your host, not the least!"

Each sip spreads whispers, adventures unfold,
Stories of blossoms, in colors so bold.
As bees take their selfies with roses in bloom,
The garden chuckles, "There's always more room!"

Bright colors are painted, these trails turn to gold,
In this sweet circus, all the secrets are told.
So join in the fun, let the nectar rain down,
In this whimsical world, wear your pollen crown!

A Celebration of Spring's Architects

Little architects buzzing, so full of glee,
Designing the blooms, oh can't you see?
With ladders of wings and blueprints of flight,
Crafting the beauty that dazzles our sight.

They plot and they plan with such grand designs,
From petals to pollen, the sweetest of lines.
"Let's put a sunflower right next to this rose,"
They giggle and pollen stick to their toes!

Each flower a project, they poke and they prod,
With a dash of sunshine, they all play the god.
"It's a garden, not just a boring old place,
Let's throw in some color, a party, a race!"

So here's to the builders, the tiny, the brave,
In gardens, they flourish, their legacy waves.
With each buzzing laugh and delightful surprise,
Spring's architects flutter under bright sunny skies!

The Unseen Hand of Nature's Artisan

Buzzing bees and shifty ants,
Crafting love with nature's chants.
A clumsy dance on petals bright,
They skip and tumble, pure delight.

Waltzing through their fragrant maze,
With silly moves, they steal the gaze.
Each flower giggles, sighs, and sways,
As lovebugs join the clumsy craze.

In gardens where the pollen flies,
These busy workers lead the ties.
Nature's jesters, all around,
Painting romance in shapes profound.

So when you smell the blooms so sweet,
Remember the dancers, light on their feet.
A cheeky wink, a fumble, a grin,
In the garden, romance does begin.

Hymn of the Trysting Flowers

Two daisies in a sunny glade,
Swaying gently while they trade.
Secrets whispered, petals blush,
Oh my, what a vibrant hush!

A rose just rolled her eyes in jest,
'Keep it down, I need my rest!'
But tulips giggle, joining in
On the cheeky floral din.

Bees, with mismatched dancing shoes,
Buzz around, sharing their views.
'Did you see that? What a show!
These flowers have their own kind of glow!'

Underneath a leafy bower,
Nature's gags unfold by the hour.
In this garden, laughter sings,
As flowers share their playful flings.

Secrets Held in the Stigma

In shadows where the petals meet,
Whispers blow on soft, warm heat.
'Who's that buzzing, creeping near?'
A bouncing bee, a hint of cheer!

'Eureka!' cries the pollen dust,
As petals giggle, bloom in trust.
Secrets known to nature's crew,
In hues of yellow, red, and blue!

With sticky fingers, artists play,
Spreading stories in a clumsy way.
A clover chuckles, twists around,
While sharing tales of love profound.

So listen close, you might just hear,
Nature's jokes that bring us cheer.
In floral hearts and buzzing beats,
All is shared, as laughter greets.

Drift of the Winged Talisman

With wings that shimmer, hover, and flit,
A flying fairy with a cheeky wit.
Drifting past where flowers bloom,
Concealing secrets, creating zoom.

A butterfly winks, adorned so bright,
'This is my stage, my ballet, my flight!'
Petals giggle, swaying in time,
As nature's revelers dance in rhyme.

'Catch me if you can!' the ladybug calls,
Looping through garden's leafy halls.
In this confetti of colors and cheer,
Nature's jesters paint the atmosphere.

So cheer for the flutters and floats, so spry,
In a world where laughter fills the sky.
With every buzz and every sway,
Nature's humor leads the play.

Whispers of the Honeyed Breeze

The bee put on a tiny hat,
Sipped nectar, then off he sat.
With pollen stuck upon his face,
He zoomed around at frantic pace.

He danced a jig upon the flower,
With moves that shocked the mini-tower.
The petals giggled, bright and bold,
As bees made stories to be told.

He buzzed a tune, a buzzing beat,
Wiggles and jiggles on his feet.
But oh, he slipped and made a splash,
In sticky honey, what a bash!

With laughter lingering in the air,
The flowers swayed without a care.
The breeze just chuckled, light as air,
As bees became the stars of flair.

Nectar's Secret Dance

In petals soft, the secrets hide,
As bees embark on a wild ride.
With flapping wings, they twist and twirl,
In sunny fields, they leap and swirl.

A flower said, 'Come do my dance!'
The bee exclaimed, 'I'll take a chance!'
He tripped on pollen, made a scene,
With fuzzy friends, they burst the sheen.

Around and round, they spun with glee,
The flowers laughed, 'Oh, can't you see?'
With nectar's charm and raucous cheer,
The buzzing troupe was far from drear.

They danced through gardens, all in sync,
With every sip, they'd pause and blink.
Then off again, a funny flight,
Their nectar dance a pure delight.

Fluttering Hearts in Blossom

In every bloom, a heart beats strong,
While fluttering friends hum their song.
A bee, in love with rosy scents,
Swam through petals, got lost in suspense.

With tango moves, he sought a queen,
Who giggled softly, what a scene!
A flower blushed, her pollen bright,
He spun around, a dancer's flight.

Together they twirled in warm air,
Giggles and buzzes filled with flair.
They made a fluttering oopsy-daisy,
And both flew off, a bit too crazy!

In every swirl, love takes the stage,
As nature writes its playful page.
In blooms they found their funny fate,
With hearts aflutter, it's never late.

The Art of Winged Wonders

Oh, the bees craft art in the air,
With tiny brushes, flitting everywhere!
They paint the flowers with sweet delight,
In funny shapes, a comical sight.

One bee tried to draw a mustache,
But got tangled in a nectar splash!
With laughter high, those flowers grinned,
While bees just giggled, gleefully pinned.

They zoomed and dashed, a buzzing crew,
Winging their way to something new.
While one made circles, oh so wide,
He forgot his lunch, but not his pride!

In the garden gallery, colors bright,
Their art took flight, a sheer delight!
So let us cheer this buzzing team,
For every bloom's their masterpiece dream!

Petal Paths and Honey Trails

Bees in suits, so slick and neat,
Buzzing 'round, what a treat!
Dancing flowers, swaying bright,
Cartwheeling blooms in pure delight.

Pollen particles on the run,
Loading up like it's all in fun!
A bee-tropolis in the sun,
Sticky fingers, oh what a pun.

A ladybug rolls by, quite fast,
Insects zooming, what a blast!
Butterflies wearing silly hats,
Tip-toe through, avoid the spats.

In this garden, laughter spills,
Nature's stage, with all its thrills.
From flower to flower, fun is near,
Join the buzz, let's all cheer!

Harmony in the Garden

Bees and blooms, a comedy,
They're in sync, oh can't you see?
Polliwogs laugh beside the pond,
Nature's charm, of this we're fond.

Worms too shy, in soil they creep,
While butterflies twirl, not a peep.
With bumblebees in flower tops,
The giggles never seem to stop.

Sunshine smiles, a bright parade,
Insects dance, the bloom brigade!
Silly shapes, they flutter by,
Waving wings as if to fly.

In this garden, joy's the theme,
Nature's antics, a lively dream.
So let's rejoice, come join the fun,
In harmony, we bloom as one!

Sipping the Golden Breath

Sip, sip, buzz, oh what a taste,
Sweet nectar flows, no time to waste!
Bees with straws, a honey spree,
Munching florals, yum, whee!

Dandelions yell, "Pick me, pick me!"
While clovers hop, "Come sip with glee!"
Pollen cakes on busy wings,
The garden's joy, oh how it sings!

Stumbling ants in clumsy lines,
Stealing sips from blooming vines.
They giggle and wiggle, what a show,
Nectar's sweet, but oh so slow!

With each buzz, a tale unfolds,
Of golden breath, of joys untold.
So raise your cups, let's make a toast,
To nature's sweets, we love the most!

Threads of Life Across the Meadow

Spreading joy on dewy threads,
Bees on bikes with flower beds!
Riding waves of fragrant fun,
Underneath the warming sun.

Bunny hops with pollen bags,
Spinning tales of flowery rags.
A ticklish breeze, a laughing flower,
Sun-kissed blooms in the bright hour.

Ladybugs play tag with flies,
Wings all flapping, oh my, oh my!
Nature's circus, what a scene,
Laughing daisies in between.

So let's all dance, in colorful style,
Wiggly worms make us smile.
In this meadow, life's a jig,
Threads of laughter, dance a big!

Murmurs in the Dance of Days

Bees in bowties buzzing round,
Sipping nectar, what a sound!
Wings a-flutter, oh so bright,
Dancing flowers, pure delight.

Ants in line, quite the parade,
Red ants think they're in a trade!
Pollen dust on their small hats,
Shuffling 'round like tiny diplomats.

Butterflies in vibrant hues,
Twirl and whirl in joyful news.
With a giggle, they alight,
Spreading joy through sheer delight.

In this garden, life's a show,
Bumbles, flutters, friend or foe?
Join the dance, come take a chance,
Nature's laughter, let's all prance!

Flames of the Colorful Wings

A ladybug with polka spots,
Tries her best to dodge the knots.
She flips and flaps on twinkling trails,
While caterpillars tell their tales.

Flutter by and hear them boast,
Of wings they've dreamt of, oh what a host!
With vibrant hues, they paint the air,
A flying circus, without a care.

With whimsical spins and twirly moves,
Bees and boogies, oh how it grooves!
Wings aflame, what a display,
In nature's color dance ballet.

Oh, what fun, amidst the blooms,
Daffodils shake off their glooms.
They giggle as they share the scene,
In a world where wings reign supreme!

Beneath the Golden Dust

Underneath the golden glow,
Pollen parties start to flow.
Buzzy bees wear tiny hats,
While deftly dodging snoozing bats.

A wise old cricket sings a tune,
Beneath a cheeky harvest moon.
Grasshoppers jump with laughter loud,
As butterflies take their proud bow.

Silly ants with crumbly treats,
Stumble on tiny dancing feet.
Who knew the garden was so grand?
With humor that's quite unplanned!

So gather 'round and join the fun,
Beneath the dust, life's never done!
Each critter winks, in verdant lands,
As nature hums with playful hands!

Lovers Under the Blooming Sky

Two butterflies on a first date,
Flapping wings while feeling fate.
Sipping nectar from a bloom,
They whisper sweet amidst the gloom.

The sun shines bright, a stage so clear,
With floral scents to endear.
A dandelion tries to peek,
Puffing seeds with a cheeky squeak.

In this garden, love does spark,
As ladybugs dance 'til it's dark.
Caterpillars laugh in a row,
With starlit giggles, hearts all aglow.

So if you see them, take a cue,
Join the dance, it's fun for you!
Under the blooms, let dreams fly high,
As lovers laugh beneath the sky!

The Secret Language of Flowers

In gardens bright, they whisper low,
"Pick me, oh pick me," to the bumblebee's glow.
With winks and nods, the daisies plot,
Their fragrant schemes, a cheeky lot.

Roses roll their eyes at tulips' flair,
"We bloom the best, but they don't care!"
Chrysanthemums giggle, under the sun,
Plotting their pranks; this bloom race is fun!

The violets snicker as the lilies prance,
"Who wore it better? Let's have a chance!"
In this floral lounge, there's joy and glee,
A secret code, just them and me.

So next time you stop and take a look,
Know they're talking, like in a book.
With smiles and laughter on silky stems,
Nature's chatters, like old friends' gems.

Nature's Gentle Couriers

The bees wear jackets made of fine fuzz,
Zooming 'round flowers, doing what does.
"Mmm honey!" they chant with glee and delight,
Their buzzing song makes the day feel bright.

Butterflies flit, with a style so bold,
"Watch my colors!" they proudly unfold.
A twirl and a swirl in the sunlight's embrace,
They jive with each flower, it's a floral race!

Ants march along, with leaves on their backs,
"We're in the game too, just cut us some slack!"
Carrying morsels from gardens so grand,
A hustle and bustle, a busy band.

And ladybugs smile, as they ride on the breeze,
"Let's play hide and seek among the tall trees!"
With all these little couriers buzzing about,
Nature's a carnival, that's what it's about!

Buzzing Joys Amidst Petals

Among the daisies, the bees bounce and glide,
"We're here for the party!" they buzz with pride.
Petals open wide with a cheeky grin,
"Join the fun, let the nectar begin!"

Whirling and twirling, a dance of delight,
Mixing the pollen, oh what a sight!
Bees trade their tales, a buzzing charade,
"I found a sweet spot!" one proudly relayed.

In fields of gold, the sunflowers sway,
"Come spin with us, it's a bloom ballet!"
Bees dip and dive, with a laugh and a cheer,
Creating a buzz that's music to hear.

As twilight falls, the beetles jump in,
"Let's celebrate flowers, let the fun begin!"
With blossoms and laughs as the day waves goodbye,
Buzzing joys linger, under evening's sky.

Nectar's Sweet Embrace

A sip of nectar, oh what a tease!
"Come taste my sweetness, I'm sure you'll please!"
The flowers wink, as the bees dive down,
Wearing their pollen like a golden crown.

"I'm the VIP of this garden show,"
Said the rose with flair, putting on a glow.
The daisies laughed, "Oh please, don't boast!"
"We all have nectar worth one big toast!"

Within the petals, a sticky affair,
Bees suckle joy with a fluttering flare.
Every drop shared, a buzzing delight,
Nature's sweet hugs wrap the day night.

So gather 'round flowers, sing loud and clear,
In nectar's sweet embrace, there's nothing to fear.
With laughter and buzzing, the fun multiplies,
In this garden of joy, where the sweetness lies.

The Veil of the Petals' Dance

In a garden bright, oh what a sight,
The bees do twirl in the soft daylight.
With pollen coats, they jump and prance,
Each flower whispers its own little dance.

They buzz with glee in their tiny suits,
Sipping nectar, their favorite fruits.
One bumps a bud, oh what a slip!
And tumbles down in a floral trip.

The blossoms giggle, swaying around,
As the bees stumble, then twirl on the ground.
In their fuzzy world, all seems so bright,
A honeyed mess is their sheer delight.

So here's to the dance of the petals so grand,
Where bees are the jesters, hand in hand.
Laughing with flowers, they make quite the show,
In the veil of their bloom, all worries should go.

Wandering Hearts of the Meadow

In a meadow wide with colors galore,
Bees wander freely, just wanting more.
On clovers and daisies, they flit without care,
With honeyed intentions, all creatures stare.

They sip like a kid at a candy store,
Buzzing with joy, who could ask for more?
One finds a petal; it looks like a hat,
He wears it with pride, a charming little brat.

The butterflies giggle, they join in the fun,
As bees chase the sun, and frolic and run.
Oh, to be a bee on this grand sunny day,
With a heart full of nectar, they're blissfully gay.

So raise up a cheer for their wandering hearts,
In gardens and meadows, they play with the arts.
With each little buzz, and flutter in flight,
They remind us of joy, like a warm sunny light.

The Language of Sweet Surrender

In a world where flowers wear scents so sweet,
Bees learn the language—now isn't that neat?
A flower's soft whisper, an open embrace,
A secretive dance in a vibrant place.

The daisies delight in the buzz of their friends,
As petals get tickled, the laughter transcends.
When one bee declares, 'This bloom is divine!'
The whole garden giggles, sipping on fine.

With nectar as bait, oh the stories they weave,
Of daring adventures, in warmth they believe.
They gather and joke, as they chill by the stem,
In the sweet orchestration, they craft a true gem.

So here's to the blooms that teach bees how to jest,
In a flowered embrace, as they buzz with the best.
Let's celebrate love in its silliest forms,
Where sweetness and laughter in nature reforms.

Honeyed Mission under the Moonlight

When the moon rises, what a curious sight,
Bees don goggles, ready for flight.
With nectar dreams leading their way,
Off on their mission, come what may.

In the twilight glow, they prosper with glee,
Laughing and stumbling, as happy as can be.
One bee miscalculates, takes a tumble or two,
But giggles abound—it's a frolicsome crew.

The stars twinkle down, whispering delight,
As bees dance around in the soft, silver light.
With nectar as treasure, they work through the night,
On a honeyed adventure, such a whimsical flight.

So toast to the bees, with their moonlit facade,
Their funny little mischiefs that leave us all awed.
In the heart of the flowers, where laughter's the boon,
The bees and the blooms keep serenading the moon.

Tapestry of Nature's Palette

In gardens bright, the bees do dance,
With tiny feet, they take their chance.
A sunflower wiggles, a daisy sighs,
While butterflies wear their best disguise.

The clovers giggle, the tulips sway,
As pollen floats like confetti play.
A bumblebee sneezes, 'Oh what a thrill!'
To sip sweet drinks, oh let's get our fill!

Lilies blush, 'We're quite a sight!'
As dragonflies zoom, hither and tight.
The hummingbirds buzz, in a wild chase,
Who knew flowers could have such a face?

With each tiny grain, they spread their cheer,
While ants march on, in straight little lines here.
Nature's a party, come join the fun,
Where nectar flows, and laughter's never done!

A Journey to the Nectar's Core

Come one, come all, to the nectar land,
Where bees do tango, and flowers stand.
With sticky feet, they make their rounds,
 In search of sweetness, joy abounds!

A ladybug rolls, with a chuckle so loud,
While the dandelions complain about crowds.
'Hey, don't sit there, it's my turn to shine!'
 'No way, that petal's just too divine!'

The ants march like they own the place,
 While worms giggle—'Oh, what a race!'
 Some petals puff with a snobby flair,
 While bees just buzz, without a care.

In sipping delight, they have a blast,
 Buzzing around, their joy unsurpassed.
Next flower, next sip, a universe awaits,
With nectar flows that dance on their plates!

Beneath the Buzzing Canopy

Beneath the green, the critters zoom,
With a flick of wings, they buzz and bloom.
Bees wear helmets, like tiny troops,
While ladybugs lead the marching groups.

A butterfly flirts, with colors so bright,
As flowers whisper, 'Oh what a sight!'
The daisies nod, in fashion so bold,
While squirrels gossip—'Did you hear the gold?'

The wind joins in, a playful tease,
Who knew nature could be such a breeze?
With pollen scattered like glitter in the air,
Even the trees pull up a chair.

A bumblebee giggles, his belly full,
He does a little dance, oh what a pull!
"Next stop, the sunset, let's paint it gold!"
And on this adventure, never feel old.

A Chorus of Fluttering Hues

In gardens alive, the colors collide,
With butterflies dancing, and bees open wide.
Each bloom has a story, a giggle to tell,
As honey drips down, all is well!

Amidst the excitement, a grasshopper sings,
While a caterpillar shows off his bling.
The tulips gossip, 'Have you seen the buzz?'
While daisies wink, 'Oh, what a fuzz!'

Bumblebees whiz by, like a wild parade,
Scattering hints of perfume they've made.
With fluttering wings, the fun never ends,
In the quirky garden where laughter blends.

Elusive, the moths with their moonlit charm,
While fireflies sparkle, in nighttime's warm.
"Join us," they call, "in this whimsical spree!"
And nature giggles—what a sight to see!

Echoes of the Pollen Path

Bumblebees dance with delight,
Tickled by petals, oh what a sight!
A flower shimmies, makes a new friend,
"Hey, come over! Let's blend!"

Yellow and fuzzy, they twirl around,
Pollen sneezes echoed all over town.
"Achoo!" said Blossom, with giggles galore,
"I may need a nap, can't take much more!"

The daisies joined in, with a chuckle bright,
"This garden party is outta sight!"
While sunbeams joined as the DJ of cheer,
Spinning tunes that the critters could hear.

Then a wind gusted in, what a silly breeze,
"Hold on tight!" yelled the flowers, "Just freeze!"
They shook and wobbled, but all held their stance,
In nature's crazy, wiggly dance!

Serenade of the Bees and Blossoms

In the garden, a buzz starts to swell,
Bees sing loudly, oh what a yell!
"Sweet nectar here, come taste and groove!"
Flowers reply with a swaying move.

A rose calls out, "Hey, I've got style!"
A lilac retorts, "Well, stick around awhile!"
The sunflowers laughed, "Don't forget our rays,
We've got the looks that could daze for days!"

Dandelions giggled, all dandy and spry,
"Catch us, dear bees! Don't let time fly by!"
But one little bee was a bit out of tune,
"Oops, wrong flower! I was looking for a prune!"

With each colorful jive, the blossoms took flight,
Bees in the middle, buzzing with might.
Together they formed a hilarious scene,
Singing their praises for pollen cuisine!

Beneath the Lavender Sky

Under skies of lavender, oh what a view,
Bees in sombreros, swaying and blue.
"You look sharp, honey!" a pansy did tease,
"Time for a fiesta, let's bust some moves!"

Zinnias sipped nectar, slurped with delight,
While daisies exchanged gossip all night.
"Did you see that bee, tripped over a rose?
He rolled in the dirt, now he's covered in prose!"

Lavender waved, trying hard not to laugh,
As a bumblebee stumbled, taking a bath.
"Artsy touch!" said Marigold, with a wink,
"Now you're a masterpiece, what do you think?"

With laughter and joy, in the garden so grand,
Pollinators danced, hand in little hand.
The fragrant comedy took the stage,
In a world where roses and bees engage!

A Kissing Wind Among the Flowers

A teasing wind blows, then shushes the leaves,
"Hey flowers, look! I'm the one who weaves!"
Petals shake, giggle, flap in a spree,
"Catch me if you can! Here comes a bee!"

Silly daisies spun in a whirl,
Demanding the winds to give them a twirl.
"Your breath is so fresh! Please dance with us now!"
Said a sunflower, with a big happy bow.

The dandelions joined, all fluffy and bright,
"Let's move it, let's groove it, it's truly a sight!"
But a gust swooped in, and they caught a chill,
Spitting seeds everywhere, what a thrill!

With the flowers all laughing, what a grand day!
For with each little gust, they were ready to play.
And as the sun set, with a wink and a grin,
Their floral fiesta was ready to begin!

Rituals of the Bright Yellow

In the garden, buzzing flies,
Dance with petals, oh what a prize!
Wiggly antennae and bright delight,
Sipping nectar, a sugary bite.

The sun is out, the blooms are bold,
Hilarious antics of green and gold.
A bumblebee stumbles, falls on his face,
While ladybugs giggle, calling it grace.

They converge in a huddle, quite a sight,
Discussing the flowers that feel just right.
Joking aside, they spread sweet cheer,
Pollinators unite, bring joy near!

In this bright haven, where laughter reigns,
With silly tricks and flowered gains.
Life's a game, everyone's in play,
From dawn till dusk, in a cheerful ballet.

Flight of the Sweet-Hearted

Oh honeybee, with your fuzzy rear,
You flit around, spreading sweet cheer.
You're the matchmaker in blooms so bright,
Finding love in petals, what a delight!

With wings a-flutter, you take to the air,
Catching the breeze without a care.
A dandelion asks, 'Why don't you stay?'
'Cause I've got dates in more flowers today!'

The butterflies tease you, calling your name,
As you zigzag through this floral game.
A rendezvous here, a dance over there,
With sweet-hearted nectar, love fills the air!

You fly in circles, doing the jig,
Bumping into blooms, oh it's quite big!
In this fun-filled chaos, you find your bliss,
In every flower's heart, a sweet little kiss.

The Gardener's Prayer

Dear plants, I pray, receive your guests,
With pollen-packed buddies, they're truly the best.
A rogue butterfly sipping, a bee on a spree,
It's a wild tea party, come join, oh me!

I scatter seeds with a hopeful grin,
Waiting for nature to bring life in.
But why do the squirrels dig like a thief?
Gardening's funny; they bring me grief!

"Help!" I shout to the bees in blue,
Your comic-timing is needed too.
Dancing around with your tiny little feet,
Cleaning my plants like it's a sweet treat.

When harvest comes, it's laughter-filled bliss,
With veggies and fruits, oh, what a miss!
Thank you, dear friends, for all your fun cheer,
My garden's alive, come year after year!

Awakening the Silent Buds

In the dawn's light, buds start to yawn,
Stretching their leaves on a crisp green lawn.
But what's that noise? A worm's silly song,
Whispered secrets all morning long.

The blossoms giggle, waking up slow,
Tickled by breezes, they're ready to grow.
'Hey, Mr. Robin, come join our line!'
It's a bloom-filled concert, a floral design!

With buzzing and flapping, the garden awakes,
As pollinators join in, oh what fun it makes!
A ladybug's waltz, a bumble's bad tune,
Who knew such laughter would blossom so soon?

So here's to the buds, with mischief in hand,
In this zany party, they surely will stand.
Nature's a riot, with splashes of hue,
In gardens of joy, there's always room for a few!

A Pollinator's Journey through Time

Buzzing around, oh what a flight,
In ancient flowers, my heart took flight.
With wings so small, yet dreams so grand,
I'm the tiny hero of this vast land.

I've seen dinosaurs munch on leaves,
While I dodged their feet with expert weaves.
History's blooms, I've known them all,
Without my work, they'd surely fall.

Fast forward now, to a garden bright,
Where humans marvel at my tiny might.
With flower hats and nectar sips,
I'm throwing floral parties, hear the tips?

In every flower, a new surprise,
With sneaky pollen, I wear my guise.
From pollen to seed, the cycle's spun,
Thanks for the tips, it's time for fun!

The Richness of Earth's Harvest

Look at me, I'm the busy bee,
Gathering goodies, feeling so free.
In fields of gold, oh what a treat,
With sweet ambition and sticky feet.

Farmers wave, their smiles so wide,
For every bloom, I'm their joyride.
I mix and mingle, it's all in the game,
Without my hustle, it's all kind of lame.

From apples to almonds, I've made the cost,
Of gardens and crops that never get lost.
With a little dance and a twirl in the air,
I'm the secret ingredient, if you dare!

So bring on the blossoms, the fruits, and the seeds,
With me on the mission, we're meeting all needs.
Together we flourish, oh what a theme,
Life's a banquet when you work as a team!

Colors in the Air

Whizzing by in a pastel swirl,
I'm a color fly, in a dreamy whirl.
With petals bright and sweets that gleam,
I'm painting the sky, oh what a dream!

Lavenders, daisies, a vibrant show,
Spilling my colors wherever I go.
Mixing hues, I'm a dancing delight,
Creating rainbows, what a sweet sight!

The tulips wave, "Come join the fun!"
While roses blush under the midday sun.
With butterflies joining my wild brigade,
We're the art team that nature made!

So here's to the flowers, let's spread some cheer,
With laughter and pollen, we shift the gear.
With nature vibrant and colors to share,
Join me, my friends, in this magical air!

The Nature of Connection

Hey there, flower, a friendly wave,
It's me, your buzz buddy, so let's be brave.
In this garden of chatter, let's draw a line,
Connecting our worlds, oh how divine!

A whiff of sweetness, I feel the pull,
With every nectar stop, my heart is full.
We share a bond, so strong and true,
A little love, and a pollen brew!

Through air we dance, no need for words,
In floral whispers, our joy is heard.
Together we flourish, no need to fret,
In this wacky dance, there's no regret.

So let's entwine, weave our spells,
In this tapestry where friendship dwells.
Nature's sweet jest, it's really quite grand,
In this wiggly world, we always stand!

The Chronicles of Earth's Benefactors

In gardens bright with blooms so fair,
Buzzing heroes skirmish through air.
With pollen pockets that weigh them down,
Workers in stripes, circling round.

Bees sip nectar, oh what a spree,
Dancing on flowers, wild and free.
But watch your step, don't squash a bee,
Or they'll tell tales of you, oh dear me!

A butterfly flutters, grace on display,
In vibrant colors, they steal the day.
But mistaking a shoe for a flower's embrace,
They'll take off like rockets, just in the race!

So let's cheer for friends with wings galore,
In the garden of laughter where we explore.
With every buzz, a humorous spin,
Thank you, dear insects, for the joy you bring!

A Blossom's Invitation

A daisy called out, "Come one, come all!
Bees, bugs, and birds, heed my sweet call!"
With petals of gold, they threw quite a bash,
But ants brought their snacks, which made a big splash.

"Fly over here!" the roses did sing,
"Bring your friends, bring your bling!"
But one bug tripped, fell flat on his face,
And the crowd burst in giggles—what a disgrace!

The lilies looked prim, all tidy and neat,
Until a blue jay dropped his lunch at their feet.
Laughter erupted, as they squawked in delight,
"I guess even flowers enjoy a good bite!"

So remember each bloom holds a wild fest,
Where nature's creatures give laughter their best.
Join the fun, be a silly little bug,
For life is a garden, all snug and snug!

Murmurs of the Pollinator's Dance

In the meadow at dawn, a bright buzz fills the air,
As insects assemble with flair and a dare.
It's the annual dance, a wild, wacky ball,
With moves so ridiculous, you'd laugh till you fall.

Bees twist and turn in a dizzying flight,
They bump and they tumble, it's quite the sight!
"Watch my new jig!" shouts a bee with a grin,
"Watch me shake pollen—Oh where did it pin?"

The butterflies flutter, with tutu-like grace,
While grasshoppers leap in a wild, zany race.
"Step aside," chirps a cricket with flair,
"My two-step's the best; do I have a spare?"

With nectar confetti falling all around,
They celebrate life in this joyful sound.
So sway with the breeze and take their chance,
Join in the fun of the insect dance!

Radiance in the Garden's Eye

In a garden alive with color and cheer,
A hummingbird zipped by, oh so near!
With a flash of his wings, he made quite a show,
As he sipped from a bloom in a quick, slick flow.

The sunflowers watched with their heads held high,
"Look at him go! What a little spry guy!"
But a gopher below, with a snack in his lap,
Chimed in loudly, "Hey buddy, don't flap!"

A ladybug chimed in, "I like to lounge,
While sipping on dew—now that's my kind of round!"
But her friend, the bumblebee, tugged on her wing,
"Come dance with us, let's have a swing!"

So under blue skies and a sun that just beams,
The garden teems with laughter and dreams.
Join the party, my friend, don't you be shy,
Dance with the bugs, under the wide open sky!

The Aroma of Wandering Souls

In fields of bloom, bees do dance,
Tickling petals, caught in a trance.
Butterflies sport their colorful threads,
While ants hold meetings on flowerbeds.

The pollen's a party, no RSVP,
Every critter's welcome, as you can see.
Bumblebees buzz with a cheerful roar,
Sipping nectar, forever wanting more!

Blossoms are hats for this grand parade,
As bees play tag in the sunlight's shade.
A sweet aroma fills the bright air,
Inviting all flowers to join the affair!

So here's to the buzzers, the fluttering crowd,
Living life loud, forever unbowed.
With laughter they spill from bloom to bloom,
In gardens alive, there's always room!

A Flutter Through Time

In a world where flowers wear glasses,
They watch as clumsy bees take passes.
With flapping wings and fuzzy heads,
They stumble and tumble, landing in beds.

Time-traveling bugs on a quest for sweet,
Zipping through history on delicious feet.
From ancient blooms to modern sprays,
They buzz with stories of fragrant days!

One bumblebee claims he met a rose,
Who whispered secrets only she knows.
He tipped his hat, all pollen-stained,
Then off to the next, his quest unchained!

So dance through the ages, oh winged brigade,
In gardens of laughter, never afraid.
With every sip, sparkles ignite,
Creating a riot in floral delight!

Songs of the Winged Weavers

With a twirl and a whir, they take to the skies,
Honey-drunk troubadours with nectar-filled sighs.
Every flower a stage, bright colors abound,
As the winged weavers flit all around.

Their tunes are sweet, filled with sunny cheer,
The croon of the bumble, the buzz we hold dear.
Melodies rise from petals in bloom,
Conducting a symphony inside every room!

Bees in tuxedos, with fancy bow ties,
Waltz past the daisies, beneath sunny skies.
They dance on the breeze, with no worries at all,
Reminding each other, we're having a ball!

So grab your partner and join the delight,
In gardens where laughter springs into flight.
With every sweet note, new stories begin,
In nature's grand concert, where we all win!

In the Heart of the Floral Realm

In a kingdom of petals, vibrant and bright,
Fluffy clouds of pollen take flight.
Flowers gossip, sharing spicy news,
As bees sneak in with their golden shoes.

Sipping tea with tulips, over affairs,
Discussing the weather and garden lairs.
A butterfly flutters, wearing a hat,
Making friends with a friendly old cat.

Fred the bee trips on a daffodil's stem,
Hoots from the daisies, "Oh, look at him!"
With laughter and giggles, they gather around,
As Fred shakes it off, with joking abound.

In this floral realm, where fun never fades,
All creatures unite in colorful raids.
So here's to the blooms, the bees, and the cheer,
In the heart of this garden, life's always near!

Swirling in the Floral Breeze

In gardens bright and wild, oh what a sight,
  Buzzing bees and butterflies in flight.
  With petals soft and colors so absurd,
They land for lunch without a single word.

  The flowers laugh, they sway with glee,
What nectar feast! Come, join the spree!
  A bee trips over, falls on a bee's knee,
    "Excuse me, sir, was that a stinger?"

  The daisies grin, they whisper jokes,
    As pollen drifts among the folks.
Bees wear shades, they know the trend,
In this sweet scene, they laugh and bend.

  The buzzing chorus sings a tune,
    A floral rave beneath the moon.
  With petals bright and spirits high,
Let's swirl and twirl 'til we're high and dry!

Guardians of the Blossoms.

In the garden, knights of pollen stand,
In capes of yellow, they rule the land.
A ladybug shouts, "Fear not the drought!"
"With my sweet umbrella, we'll never pout!"

The bees all buzz, with wings like swords,
Dancing through petals, they're never bored.
They sip on nectar, bold and brave,
While ants march in line, like they're on a rave.

A butterfly swoops with a flip and a flap,
"Oh, look! A toadstool! Let's take a nap!"
But the daisies giggle, "Wake up, sleepyhead!"
"Or you'll miss the party that blooms ahead!"

With laughter and cheer, they guard the way,
Mixing sweet scents, come join the fray!
In this realm of flowers, oh what a sight,
Where guardians of blossoms party all night!

Whispers of the Willow's Wing

Willow branches sway like a graceful dance,
As whispers flit, give the bugs a chance.
A tiny bee asks, "Am I too late?"
"Nonsense! Join us now for a pollen date!"

The wind holds secrets, soft and sweet,
As nature spins yarns beneath our feet.
A grasshopper jokes, "I'm not in the mood!"
The flowers chime in, "Let's brighten your brood!"

They gather 'round, sharing stories galore,
With petals as pillows, they dream and explore.
A whisper of humor floats through the air,
The feet of a beetle try dancing with flair!

As twilight descends, a glow fills the glade,
With giggles and joy, no plans ever made.
In willow's embrace, let the laughter soar,
As whispers of joy leave you wanting more!

Dance of the Dandelion Dreams

In fields of gold, the dancers convene,
With dandelions twirling, a sight so serene.
A puffball leaps, with a kick and a fling,
"Catch me, if you can! Come join the spring!"

The breeze takes charge, a partner in crime,
While bees spin around in a wiggly rhyme.
"Is this the dance of the dandelions?"
Everyone giggles, including the pythons!

Fluffy seeds take flight, like wishes on air,
Tickling the clouds, they don't have a care.
"Oh, where do you go?" a flower inquires,
"Off to the moon! To fuel cosmic fires!"

And while the stars twinkle, the daisies sway,
As the dandelion dreams twirl and play.
With laughter and cheer, they light up the night,
In this dance beneath the moon, oh what a sight!

In the Arms of the Blossoming Trees

Bees in ballet, they twirl and dive,
Buzzing around, oh, what a jive!
Pollen everywhere, a yellow spree,
Nature's little dancers, wild and free.

Silly flowers, wearing bright hats,
Shaking their petals, looking like cats.
"Come dance with us!" the daisies say,
While the bees giggle, "We're on our way!"

A ladybug joins, a wobbly twirl,
Spinning on petals, giving a whirl.
A chorus of laughter from all around,
In this funny world, no frown can be found.

In this blooming club, drinks are sweet,
Nectar cocktails, quite the treat!
With every sip, they laugh and sing,
In the arms of trees, what joy they bring!

Harvest of the Winged Messengers

Flapping and buzzing, what's that sound?
Winged messengers swarming all around.
With tiny briefcases, they toil and zoom,
In their floral office, chaos and bloom.

"Time for a meeting!" the butterflies boast,
"Who knew work could be such a roast?"
Dropping sweet secrets, they giggle and play,
Retrieving sweet treats from work every day.

Hummingbirds hover, sipping with flair,
"Watch us, dear friends, we defy the air!"
Their tiny speedboats whizz past the tulips,
Leaving behind a trail of flower tips.

Soon comes the sunset, their workday ends,
With pollen in pockets, oh how it blends!
"Until tomorrow!" they shout with glee,
Harvesting laughter from flower to tree!

Whirlwind in a Meadow's Song

A breeze plays a tune, the flowers sway,
Singing and spinning, come join the play!
A whirlwind of petals, where joy takes flight,
In a meadow so bright, what a funny sight!

Bees in hard hats, they haul and lift,
Transporting sweet bundles, a busy gift.
"Don't drop that nectar!" a bumblebee shouts,
As daisies and tulips jiggle about.

Grasshoppers join in with a tap and hop,
Making the melody go nonstop.
Who knew a meadow could throw such a bash?
Where butterflies flutter and crickets clash!

With laughter and pollen, a feast of the day,
The whole crew gathers to dance and sway.
A whirlwind of joy in this nature's song,
In the heart of the meadow, where all belong!

Gossamer Wings and Floral Whispers

Whispers in petals, a fluttering sound,
Gossamer wings dancing round and round.
"Excuse me!" says one, with a giggly sweep,
"Did you smell that? It's quite a leap!"

Bees jive in the sun, with sunglasses on,
Buzzing and buzzing, from dawn till dawn.
"Pollen party!" they cheer with delight,
While daisies and roses keep the vibe right.

In this floral banquet, sweet sips abound,
Giggling bees sipping, not making a sound.
They raise tiny toasts, "To nectar divine!"
And the daisies dance in a line, line, line!

With each little buzz, the fun never ends,
Floral friends gathering, the joy extends.
In this garden of humor, so bright and gay,
Gossamer wings lead the dance all day!

www.ingramcontent.com/pod-product-compliance
Lightning Source LLC
Chambersburg PA
CBHW071814160426
43209CB00003B/87